ALTERED
STATES

ALTERED
STATES

GLOBALIZATION,

SOVEREIGNTY,

AND GOVERNANCE

GORDON SMITH, CANADA

Chairman, Board of Governors, International Development Research Centre

MOISÉS NAÍM, VENEZUELA

Editor, Foreign Policy, *Carnegie Endowment for International Peace*

INTERNATIONAL DEVELOPMENT RESEARCH CENTRE

Ottawa • Cairo • Dakar • Johannesburg • Montevideo • Nairobi • New Delhi • Singapore

Published by the International Development Research Centre
PO Box 8500, Ottawa, ON, Canada K1G 3H9
http://www.idrc.ca

© Better World Fund, United Nations Foundation 2000

Canadian Cataloguing in Publication Data

Smith, Gordon S.

Altered states: globalization, sovereignty and governance /
Gordon Smith and Moisés Naím

ISBN 0-88936-917-8

1.   Legitimacy of governments
2.   International economic relations
3.   Democracy
4.   Sovereignty
I.   Title.
II. Naím, Moisés
III. International Development Research Centre (Canada)

JC327.S64 2000   320.1/01   C00-900064-X

IDRC Books endeavours to produce environmentally friendly
publications. All paper used is recycled as well as recyclable.
All inks and coatings are vegetable-based products.

TABLE OF CONTENTS

Globalization challenges and reinforces the power of the state.
Governance is tested in a turbulent confusion of opportunity,
insecurity, and anxiety. The Millennium Assembly of the
United Nations offers the chance for productive debate
on how humankind will govern itself in the global village.

What do the World Bank, Microsoft, and Greenpeace have in
common? The noisy town square of world politics is populated
by all manner of nonstates. Part 1 explores how failures of
governance are related to pressures of globalization. It then
suggests how governments might respond to urgent problems
of peace and security, social equity, and protecting the
global environment.

Preventing deadly conflict, providing opportunities for the
young, and managing climate change — three urgent obligations
of governance. Part 2 examines these imperatives in their complex
dimensions: South–North; foreign–domestic; public–private.
Practical recommendations for improved governance are
proposed for the consideration of the Millennium Assembly.

Conclusion

GOVERNING PRINCIPLES:
THE UNITED NATIONS AND THE MILLENNIUM ASSEMBLY   61

Globalization demands that we develop new forms of governance. And, as a natural nexus to the growing global networks of governance, the United Nations can lead in this process. Just as in 1944 at Bretton Woods, in Manhattan at the turn of the millennium, we can seize the opportunity to reconstruct our future.

Appendices

FOREWORD

As crowds of protesters and clouds of tear gas dispersed from the site of last year's World Trade Organization summit in Seattle, one thing was clear. There is great alarm and anger over the forces shaping our world. Although globalization offers many opportunities, it is also blamed for many ills. But as members of the international community, we can take advantage of globalization's benefits to counter its negative effects. Flashpoints of conflict, the degraded environment, and the vast gap between rich and poor are all global problems that demand joint action based on mutual interests and facilitated by near-instant communication.

The International Development Research Centre (IDRC) believes that the United Nations is the forum to address these challenges. But to be an effective forum, the UN needs to find itself at the centre of improved global governance. The authors of *Altered States* propose such an agenda for the UN Millennium Assembly, to be held in September 2000.

As the convenor of the Friends of the United Nations, IDRC has been delighted to help in the preparation of this report, commissioned by the Better World Fund, sister organization of the United Nations Foundation. With 30 years of support to research in developing countries, IDRC has a long-standing interest in the United Nations and a shared commitment of creating a just, equitable, and safe world.

This common aim finds voice in a phrase of Hannah Arendt from *On Violence*: "Power corresponds to the human ability not just to act but to act in concert." IDRC's work with partners in the South to identify and solve development problems has put acting with others at the core of our mission. It is with this vision that we call for global governance expressed in discourse rather than division, collaboration rather than conflict, action rather than apathy.

Maureen O'Neil
President, International Development Research Centre

PREFACE

To those who see a certain immodesty in an essay purporting to describe most of what is wrong with governance on Earth, we have an answer: It wasn't our idea. This project was imagined and commissioned in 1999 by the United Nations Foundation and its Better World Fund. It owes everything to the wisdom and continuing support of Ted Turner, Chairman of the Board of the United Nations Foundation; Maurice Strong, Chairman of the Executive Committee; and Tim Wirth, President. Indeed, our work began when the latter two together telephoned one of us (Smith) with the invitation to re-envision the UN as a contribution to preparations for a UN Millennium Summit. It was an irresistible proposition, but our report is only one element of a timely and extensive examination of governance, global issues, and the United Nations that the Foundation has sponsored. In all modesty, this report is a product of the urgency, commitment, and (we dare say) courage that define the important work of the UN Foundation.

Our first intention is to promote a much wider, global discussion of the great costs and confusions of globalization – and of the rich opportunities still to be realized. Generating that discussion is not a vain or pious hope: one of the powerful dynamics of globalization, and perhaps in the end its saving virtue, is a potential democratization of global politics. All readers are therefore invited to keep the conversation going, to let us hear your thoughts. We are convinced, as we say in our report, that all of us on the globe must learn to govern better together, or we will fail to govern at all – with catastrophic results.

The experience of preparing our report has also persuaded us (notwithstanding some skepticism of our own about the efficacy of the present organization) that a stronger and more effective United Nations is a precondition of good governance on Earth. It is trite to repeat, but true, that the UN would need inventing if it didn't already exist. What is less comfortably recognized is that the past practice and bad habits of UN politics, if left uncorrected, will very likely condemn us to a future of messy disasters. If we are to rescue ourselves and our children from deadly conflict, from poverty, illness, and violence among the young, from the many menaces of climate change – if we are to govern ourselves better – we must improve the UN.

To that end, our report is addressed particularly to heads of government (and to those who give them advice) as they prepare to assemble for a UN Millennium Summit in September 2000. Most of what ails the UN reflects failures of political leadership and political agreement. It lies in the power of the leaders assembling in September either to make the UN or to break it. We think we have advanced some practical, necessary measures and procedures that will allow the summit to succeed. At the least, we hope to have facilitated the preparations of Secretary-General Kofi Annan.

We know that some will say there is nothing new here, and that our recommendations in the main restate the obvious. It is true we have displayed no magic; instead, we hope to have advanced the powerful logic of collaborative action.

Our best insights were not our own. We exchanged information and queried some 40 contributors around the globe and guiltlessly adopted some of their best ideas. We have deeply appreciated the enduring counsel of Louise Fréchette and of John Ruggie, whose advice we hope has strengthened the relevance of what we have written. We are furthermore the beneficiaries of the "Friends of the UN Vision Project." They have generously shared their advice and their warnings, and have significantly shaped our views (but should not be held accountable for any part of our report).

Many others have helped us in this endeavour, and the report is significantly better as a result. We are especially indebted to David Angell, Richard Butler, Sir Marrack Goulding, David Malone, Adil Najam, Francisco Sagasti, Michele Wingelman, and Mark Zacher.

We are grateful to John Hay, whose drafting gave expression to our ideas and to many of his own. And we are obliged to the people of the International Development Research Centre, who have managed the publication and distribution of our work.

Finally (and even if we embarrass him by so doing) we thank Paul Isenman, formerly of the UN Foundation and the Better World Fund. This project would not have been undertaken without him. He has been a wonderful partner, encouraging and wise. He carries our best wishes to his new activities at the Organisation for Economic Co-operation and Development.

Gordon Smith [gordonssmith@home.com]
Moisés Naím [mnaim@ceip.org]
January 2000

EXECUTIVE SUMMARY

The world needs new ways of governance. We know this because the old ways are failing. True, human progress is evident in many realms. But complacency is dangerous. Too many people are poor, and millions have become poorer in the past 10 years. Income disparities are growing much worse. The world's population increases at intimidating rates, most of all in the poor countries. Deadly conflicts cause appalling misery, even when they could be – should be – prevented; weapons of mass destruction threaten us all. The climate, the very future of life on Earth, is changing. These are the failures that compel us to improve the ways we govern ourselves.

They are failures, in the main, to mitigate the damage and inequities of globalization – and to seize its opportunities. "Globalization" itself has become a term so over-used and abused that it often defies definition. Some see globalization as the mask of Americanization. Others argue that it describes nothing new: after all, countries and cultures have always affected one another, not least by trade and invasion. But the current wave of international integration and interdependence is different. The connections and their effects, between people and states, are not just more numerous and profound but transforming. They change how we live, how we will have to govern, in ways still not fully understood.

The dynamics of this globalization are multifaceted and seemingly contradictory. In some respects they undermine the power of states. The power of transnational corporations, the limits imposed on government policy by currency markets, the transborder politics of NGOs, the transfiguring power of global media – all reduce the autonomy of national governments. But in other respects, globalization strengthens the state and extends its influence: in the international protection of human rights or in the cooperation that states undertake to preserve the oceans, eradicate disease, subdue the contagion of financial shocks, or stabilize global warming. Sovereignty is not what it used to be. It is more. And it is also less.

Where globalization confounds governance, and stirs conflict, is in its turbulent tendency not only to integrate countries and societies but also to fracture them – in the politics of secession, and in the divisions of generation, tribe, and belief. Some teenage citizens of a global Nintendoland feel more affinity with each other than with their own parents or neighbours. Nowhere is the strife more sorely felt than in the contests of culture, seen by many in the world as a struggle of Hollywood vs diversity, consumerism vs identity.

In sum, good governance requires first a recognition of three key issues of the present globalization:

- *Interests* – Globalization does not operate primarily as an inevitability, either of nature or of history. Many of the forces of globalization are driven by powerfully motivated interests, both private and public, which any practical attempts at better governance must acknowledge.
- *Equity* – For all the opportunities it creates, globalization has also deepened pre-existing inequalities. The interdependence of globalization is dramatically asymmetric: while some prosper by it, others suffer. Better governance means a better distribution of globalization's costs and benefits.
- *Governance itself* – Globalization breaks down states, but it can also build them up. It confines autonomy. But for the great purposes of governance – securing the peace, alleviating poverty, creating an equitable social harmony, protecting the environment – globalization endows states with new capacities and a new legitimacy for action far beyond national borders.

A defining characteristic of the present globalization is that it defeats the attempts of states to manage on their own. No state, not even the superpower, can by itself protect its people from conflict, climate change, the debilitating influences of the drug trade, or the upheavals caused by financial crises half a world away. We all now inhabit a planet on which our worst problems are shared problems. They demand cooperative solutions – states collaborating with each other, and with institutions, NGOs, businesses and others, in the fluid alliances that now mark the ways we govern best.

No effort of governance will succeed (nor should it) if it is not sufficiently democratic. People are entitled by right to some meaningful say in the institutions that govern their lives, be it their own legislature or the World Trade Organization. In fact, the globalization of communication and action arms citizens with the information and the means they need to give consent, and sometimes to refuse it. Better governance, by definition, means more transparency, more accountability, and a more popular participation in the decisions that count.

To illustrate some of the dangerous failures of governance, we point to three global challenges and the imperatives for action: preventing deadly conflict, providing opportunities for the young, and managing climate change. These are three of the urgent themes that should confront government leaders around the world as they prepare for the 2000 Millennium Summit of the United Nations in New York.

We are acutely aware of the many barriers to progress, from interests to ideology to institutional weakness. But we are even more aware of the hazards in a "peaceful coexistence" with the status quo, the futility of evading problems on the excuse that they look intractable. We know that our own proposals can be dismissed as naive. But we are convinced that it is even more naive to believe nothing can be done.

- **To prevent deadly conflict** – whether between countries or within them, or in the borderless menace of terrorism – demands a new and wiser understanding of the developing norm of humanitarian intervention. But it also requires immediately achievable reforms in United Nations operations: enhanced authority for the Secretary-General to warn of impending conflict; restricted great-power use of their Security Council vetoes; and enhanced UN capacity to deploy police, peacekeepers, and (if need be) fighting troops to prevent or suppress bloody conflicts and then to rebuild peace.

- **Providing opportunities for the young** – and for a global population expected to rise to 8 billion from 6 billion in the next 25 years – requires a similarly pragmatic set of immediate actions: rescuing children from the plague of HIV/AIDS; enrolling every young child in basic education; expanding access to the Internet, especially in the poor countries; and adopting tough (and profitable) new measures to protect children's health – by the international control of tobacco and by phasing out the sale of leaded gasoline.

- **Managing the many harms of climate change** represents both a collective obligation and a rich opportunity. Success will turn on a grand bargain between rich countries and poor – a global strategy of reducing greenhouse-gas emissions while promoting accelerated and sustainable development. The design of that bargain is already in place, agreed at the Rio Earth Summit and in the 1997 Kyoto Protocol. Needed now is will – and action.

The UN belongs at the centre of these necessary new
approaches. It is already a nexus for the public–private networks
of deliberation and governance, and a unique source of
legitimacy for decision and action. That is why the Millennium
Assembly and its summit in 2000 represent an extraordinary
opportunity – a time to redirect the powerful energies of
globalization for a shared and better future.

INTRODUCTION
GLOBALIZATION: HOPES AND WARNINGS

Jacques Delors looked dumbfounded. A statesman of skilled
sophistication, he seemed nonetheless incredulous when he
was asked one day in Montréal if sovereignists were not "in the
vanguard" of global change — invited, in other words, to identify
Québec's separatists with the progress of history. As president still
of the European Commission, one of the architects of Europe's
own integration, Delors managed a response to the effect that
sovereignty as once understood was now an abstraction of
doubtful relevance. It was a brief exchange but telling, because
it spoke directly to the turbulence of a world tensed between
globalism and localism, and to the confusions and frustrations
of governance everywhere.

That dangerous turmoil is plain to see, evident in the everyday
difficulties and frequent failures of governments. Economic
insecurity, polluted environments, the restless loyalties of the
young, brooding conflicts of tribe and territory: all confound the
capacity even of the most powerful state to govern alone, even in
its own country. Not only do states strain to cope with the forces
of globalization, they cannot even resolve many of their own
troubles at home.

In truth, the character of the state itself is in doubt — its capacity
challenged, its legitimacy contested. Again the evidence is
familiar: huge transnational corporations, nongovernmental
organizations, intergovernmental organizations, global media
and multitudes of others, all lay claim to authority that states once
called their own. And failures are debilitating. If people come to
believe that states cannot improve economies or supply adequate
schooling or administer justice, they will assign their loyalties
(and their resources) elsewhere — inward to local institutions and
movements, or outward to transnational alternatives. When that
happens, state capacity is again diminished, legitimacy is lost, and
power seeps away.

But even as the state is disparaged and weakened, it is reinforced
simultaneously with new powers and higher expectations.
Internally, fear of globalization's powerful effects drives people
to the refuge and reassurance of the institutions they know — to
shelter their cultures, to protect their economies, or simply to
have a say in their increasingly uncertain futures. Externally,
the state is strengthened as governments collaborate to extend
their influence across frontiers and around the world. Even as
countries undergo domestic division, they connect with each
other more closely in transborder communities of shared
endeavour. The eradication of a terrible disease by a United
Nations vaccination program, the moderation of a currency
crisis by the (just-in-time) intervention of central bankers, a
new treaty to conserve high-seas fisheries — these are all actions of
states, expressions of state sovereignty, facilitated by globalization.

What becomes more obvious, however, is the troubling mismatch between the institutional capacities and customs of governance and the problems that need solving. We are simply not organized well to manage our affairs. This is why the dynamics of globalization inspire such dread and resistance, whether among Swiss farmers afraid for their livelihoods, or suddenly unemployed South Koreans, aboriginal peoples tenacious in defence of their cultures, or worried Illinois teachers with pensions invested in rickety Asian securities.

It is an irony, moreover, that the autonomy and capacity of states have come to be doubted just when most of the world's people for the first time live in democracies (generously defined). After surviving the long progress to democratic government, men and women have won a disturbingly ambiguous prize: responsible government, yes, but responsible for what? Capable of what? If there is a power shift that now disfavours the state, what is the remaining significance of democratic government? Can states any longer govern? Can globalization be democratized?

These questions form the subject of this report. We explore the dynamics of globalization, and discuss what makes today's globalization different from earlier kinds. We test the prevailing wisdom about sovereignty and state capacity (and sort out the humbug). We consider whether sovereignty itself is an impediment or a requirement to security and prosperity. And, in three urgent areas ripe for progress (preventing deadly conflict, providing opportunities for the young, and managing the many harms of climate change), we advance plans of action by which states, with others in the global community, can govern successfully in the future. The message here is meant to give both hope and warning. Globalization opens great possibilities of prosperity, security, and human well-being, but only if we construct new ways of governance.

This is why the opening of the new millennium, for some just a mark on Christendom's calendar, can be seized as an opportunity for all. The Millennium Assembly, convened at the United Nations in the fall of 2000, can itself constitute an exercise in good governance – in which "We, the peoples of the United Nations," through our governments and in the quickening activities of civil society, adopt pragmatic and collaborative reforms. If we are to reconstruct the ways we govern ourselves, the UN is the necessary and fitting place to start.

PART 1

SOVEREIGNTY AND GLOBALIZATION: GOVERNMENT IN A STATE OF CONFUSION

Globalization has already inspired an immense and expanding literature, some of it useful. Our purpose is not to enlarge it; we advance no Theory of Everything, no bold prediction. Instead, the attempt here is to detect connections between globalization and failures of governance, and then to suggest possible courses of action, by governments and others, on some specific and pressing issues.

A new kind of global community is forming, making the present and future different from the past. The facts of interconnectedness are well known and unavoidable, in the statistics of trade and investment, in the diffusion of conflict from country to country, in the shared vulnerability to poisoned air or encroaching drought — and in the fearful antipathies of culture and commerce, identity and technology, democracy and the market. At war or peace, we are more neighbours than ever, like it or not.

Granted, countries and cultures have always affected one another, not least by trade and invasion. But the character of the present globalization is different, in kind and in degree. The connections and their effects between states and between people are not only more numerous but also transforming. They change the ways we live, the ways we will have to govern. To begin to see the transformations, look at the apparent paradox. Set against the disrupting forces of globalization are the equally turbulent features of fragmentation: secessions and partitions, the fretted cleavages of generation, ethnicity and aspiration, and the sense even in the rich democracies of alienation, disparity, and inequity. At the same time that cultural affinities and technology (especially cheap, fast communications and travel) draw people together across boundaries, new definitions of identity and interest drive people apart within borders.

How to accommodate these seemingly contrary tendencies? In fact, they are two sides of the same phenomenon. Fragmentation and integration are one: "fragmegration" in the apt if unmusical invention of political scientist James Rosenau. Basque secessionists try to make common cause with Scottish Nationalists. Malaysian teenagers feel more in common with Swedes their age (fellow citizens of Nintendoland) than with their own Malaysian parents. Environmental movements arise locally, but can act globally in coalition with like-minded NGOs and foreign governments anywhere on the planet — all exchanging email intimacies of common strategy and shared values.

Nowhere is the tension between globalism and localism felt more sorely than in the passionate struggles of culture. By the mid-1990s, Benjamin Barber had found the sense of it in his *Jihad vs. McWorld*: "Caught between Babel and Disneyland, the planet is falling precipitously apart and coming reluctantly together at the very same moment." To which Barber added a second insight: in the realm of culture, "globalism" to most people usually means

"Americanism." "Its template is American" as Barber put it. "Its goods are as much images as materièl, an aesthetic as well as a production line. It's about culture as commodity, apparel as ideology." And for many outside the United States, the dynamic of cultural globalism is not a benign competition for market share. It is a struggle between predator and prey, dominance and diversity. Whether in the defiance of Taliban clerics, or the cunning of the Quai d'Orsay defending the cultural industries of France, the culture wars are fought with a desperate intensity.

THREE CRUCIAL ISSUES OF GLOBALIZATION

1. Interests

Globalization is sometimes about immutable nature – a tragic earthquake in Turkey or Taiwan that compels worldwide sympathy and attracts an international response. More often, globalization is about actions and behaviours more or less deliberately arrived at. Interests, more than chance or nature, propel much of globalization's dynamics. Nike organizes the global manufacture and marketing of shoes to achieve corporate objectives. Governments deregulate markets, float exchange rates and otherwise yield control to global markets to achieve (successfully or not) their economic objectives. The Hollywood entertainment industry – the largest export industry in the United States – attacks the defences of cultural protectionism wherever it encounters them, generally with the supporting fire of US government trade authorities. The NGOs that exploited the Internet so famously to forge coalitions with governments for the landmines treaty were globalizing just as avidly as Burger King or Mitsubishi. The NGOs that rallied against the OECD's aborted Multilateral Agreement on Investment, the MAI, exploited globalism even as they condemned it. (The local revolt in southern Mexico explains its grievances in the context of global economics. For their critique of modern globalism, click on http://www.ezln.org, official website of the Zapatistas.)

Of course, the East India Company of the 17th century was also a powerful globalizer in pursuit of interests. But that was different. Technologies of production and transportation, and especially of communication, endow General Motors (or organizers of Internet rock concerts) with a global reach and effect unimaginable in earlier eras.

This is not to say that the consequences of globalization are always intended by these diligent globalizers. (The global auto industry no more intends global warming than it intends traffic jams.) It only asserts the obvious but commanding fact: many of the most significant forces of globalization are driven by powerfully motivated interests – both private and public – which any practical attempt at governance will have to acknowledge.

2. Equity

Globalization has carried with it a remarkably uneven distribution of costs and benefits. The result, for the most part, has been to exacerbate inequalities of wealth, consumption, and power within and between countries. It may be a truism that globalization entails interdependence, in the sense that what happens in one country is influenced by what happens in another. But the interdependence is dramatically asymmetric: some are more vulnerable than others. And while some prosper by globalization, many others suffer from it. The prosperers embrace globalization and speed it along. But among the losers, and those who fear to lose, globalization generates opposition and despair.

More than 80 countries have per-capita incomes lower now than a decade or more ago; the gap between the rich countries and the poor grows worse. The income ratio between the fifth of the world's people in the richest countries and the fifth in the poorest was 30 to 1 in 1960, and 60 to 1 in 1990; by 1997, it had grown to 74 to 1. Far from financing a convergence of fortunes between rich and poor people, globalization has coincided with a decade of increasing concentration of income, wealth, and control over resources. OECD countries, with 19 percent of the global population, account for 71 percent of world trade, 58 percent

In all this confusion it gets harder to tell whether states should be expected to do more and more, or less and less. The enigmatic answer: both more and less. Here is why:

One of the chief characteristics of these globalizing dynamics is that they overwhelm the attempts of states to manage globalization alone or control its effects. Examples abound in economics, in the prevention of conflict, in the protection and restoration of the environment. Even in the smallest details of domestic legislation and regulation, every state is now constrained by international norms, law, political obligation, and opinions in world markets. (To raise a government's revenues, for example, or to propose a government expenditure, is first to judge the tolerance of the global bond market and the mood swings of currency traders.) Meanwhile, the transcending, supranational issues of peace, development, and the preservation of the planet defy resolution by states applying old rules and old tools in old institutions.

No state by itself can protect its people from conflict or climate change or the incendiary pressures of population growth, not even a superpower. The loss of autonomy is readily measured
- By the intrusive intensity of global trade, communications, and other transactions;
- By the widening extent and variety of these interconnections across every aspect of life;
- By the sheer velocity of action and reaction, now calibrated at the speed of laser through fibre-optic cable; and
- By the effects of all these connections, felt deep inside economies, societies, and even psyches.

We all now inhabit a planet on which our worst problems are shared problems. They demand cooperative solutions. It's not that states are no longer important; it's that autarky is no longer possible, or affordable. The old ways of governance do not work, and the ruinous failures are everywhere evident – in the backward course of de-development in many of the poorest countries; in wars fought by boy soldiers, chopping the hands off infant victims; in the contagion of currency crises; in the ominous collapse of corals from the Caribbean to the South Pacific; in the altered chemistry of the climate itself.

But if the failures are so obvious, why do they recur? If globalization compels us all to change how we govern domestically and globally, what stands in the way? Two things, mostly: habits of mind and the inertia of interests. Together, they explain the dangerous and costly mismatch between existing institutional capacity and the demands placed on that capacity at all levels of government.

Habits of mind? Most of us are inclined to think of the state as the natural and predominant unit of the "international system" (itself an expression that misleads us to think of order and equilibrium). We take for granted, as static facts and even when we know better, old assumptions of sovereignty, autonomy, and impermeable borders. This is risky imagery, rooted in a past far different from the present. And in its frequent failure to

explain current realities, it encourages an easy defeatism. When well-armed, well-off states hang back from even the humblest of humanitarian intervention for lack of normative guidance, or shrink from even the cheapest and surest treaty of mutual environmental protection, when the veto states on the Security Council recoil from confronting even a true threat to global peace and security, more failures follow. Worse, these attitudes of defensiveness and retreat block long-term strategic thinking in favour of short-term temporizing and electoral manoeuvre. The result, with lamentable frequency, is a failure to undertake the institutional, financial, and political reforms that effective governance requires.

Inertia of interests? Let us acknowledge again that considerable numbers of powerful people are flourishing in the current circumstance: those who sit comfortably in the prevailing institutions, and particularly those who are selling what the world is buying. To repeat: globalization is not entirely an inevitable force, either of nature or of history, even if many of its consequences are unintended. Its processes and values are not all automatic or self-perpetuating. The present conditions of life reflect in some degree the actions and reactions of firms, organizations, and governments (all interacting) whose leaders (albeit with different aims) see their interests thereby served.

There is nothing new in the phenomenon of multiple uncoordinated decisions producing (for many) unexpected harm. That is what market crashes, over-fishing, and mutations of drug-resistant microbes are all about. What the present globalization has introduced, along with its wealth of opportunity, is a new extent, a new intrusiveness — and a new destructiveness — in the harm done.

Dysfunctional habits of mind and a lively concern for self-interest are not peculiar to world politics; they work just as powerfully inside countries. The difference is that successful states institutionalize interest accommodation and compromise, including the compromise between long-term solutions and short-term politics. And this brings us to the practical benefits of democratic process. Democratic politics are understood by the strength of their procedures for holding the powerful accountable to the rest. This is the unifying virtue of democratic

governments – not that they invariably do the right thing, but that they are held responsible when they do the wrong thing, with procedures for their peaceful replacement.

But in global politics, how is the World Bank genuinely accountable to the millions of people it helps or hurts? How effectively is the Security Council held accountable? Or Microsoft? Or Greenpeace? Another question (just as worrying) is whether there is a contradiction between the liberating, wealth-making free-market impulse of economic globalization and the values of democratic governance.

Many people take the view that the ascendant values of the unregulated market militate against values of democratic governance. This is the fear, widespread and intensely felt, that inspires such angry sentiment against the World Trade Organization: the belief that the WTO institutionalizes dominant market values, "commodifies" life, and operates immune from citizen participation. The market fosters inequalities, these critics argue, while democracy rests on equal rights and shared resources; the market encourages selfishness, democracy calls for self-restraint and compromise. In this contest of values, they warn, it has been the market prevailing over democracy.

Whether or not they are right, there is a strong ethical and functional case for bringing greater democracy into the institutions of global governance. The ethical argument is straightforward: people are entitled, as a right, to some meaningful say in the conduct of the institutions that govern their lives. When the national government was practically the only institution that mattered in governance, a voice in choosing that government might have sufficed. Not so when the International Monetary Fund or Mercosur starts making the rules.

The functional argument for transparency and accountability is equally important. No institution of authority now can long endure without the informed consent of those who are governed by it. Globalization itself is arming people with the information

they need to give consent and, in some cases, the means to refuse it – think of worldwide consumer boycotts promoted on television and coordinated on the Internet. But lack of democratic processes is keeping international institutions weak, and for a very good reason. People living in democracies are understandably reluctant to transfer allegiance and power to organizations less accountable (and even more remote) than their own national governments. And finally, no institution is likely to make smart decisions if it doesn't bear a duty to explain them to someone. Remember the OECD's embarrassment of blunders in its too-secret negotiation of the failed MAI.

As many have remarked, much that we already know about globalization is recognizably American. Here, for instance, is how Daniel F. Burton (a vice-president at Novell) described the Internet in the Spring 1997 issue of *Foreign Policy*: "The Internet is already home to a kind of Wild West ethos that is often associated with new frontiers. It is antiauthoritarian, vehement in its defence of individualism and free speech, radical in its concern for privacy, and, for the most part, extremely antigovernment." These traits are immediately seen by everyone else for what they are: as American as MTV, Levis, or Intel. This belies the notion that the new technologies are culture neutral; they aren't. As well, it should demonstrate to Americans – even to American isolationists – that they have more invested than anyone else in the successful governance of global affairs.

The United States owes its pre-eminence in the world not primarily (if at all, some would say) to its unique military capabilities. The present wealth and political influence of the United States spring from the universal appeal of some of its founding ideals, from the economic success that size and a peaceful continent allowed, and from a zealous exploitation of international trade and investment. Americans have more money invested abroad than anyone else. They export more than anyone else. They define their own political and economic interests more expansively than anyone else.

Some Americans will mutter that they also pay more than anyone else in military budgets, UN dues, and foreign aid of all varieties. Quite so, but that only underlines the truth. The people of the United States have more to gain than anyone else from better governance of the world's problems: secure markets; safe foreign investments; the timely prevention of foreign conflicts; an efficient distribution of risk among states when it comes to sending forces to war; a healthy natural environment; a broadly shared international prosperity, with a continuing demand for goods and services (and values) "Made in the USA."

The United States has clear and present interests in developing an effective UN, in international policies addressing the coming hardships of population growth, in concerted action against catastrophic climate change. But they are interests not always reflected in US policy. Still less are these interests reflected in congressional votes. As a case in point, the US Senate's wrong-headed rejection of the Comprehensive Test Ban Treaty harks back to an isolationism that cannot not serve the United States any less disastrously in the future than it did in the past. Polls of US public opinion uniformly confirm that most Americans see the wisdom of sharing burdens through the UN and other institutions (the more so when they are told how little it costs them). Yet dithery policy and tireless scapegoating of the UN persist, destructively. They play into the vicious circle of underfunding and disappointing performance that weakens the UN's operations and its reputation. Every turn of that circle damages US interests.

The case for better governance is therefore directed to the people of the United States as much as to anyone. To meet the great challenges facing you requires collaboration with others: other governments, other peoples, other institutions. Unilateralism will prove as futile as isolationism. You cannot protect your security, your prosperity, or the air you breathe or the water you drink without the cooperation of others. Nobody, not even the superpower, can go it alone. In the present age (to adapt an insight of Hannah Arendt), power does not ordinarily mean bringing force to bear; more practically, power is the capacity to act with others in pursuit of agreed objectives.

That is most clearly true in the realm of global public goods — productive oceans, good air, exchange-rate tranquility — all the many goods that the people of any country enjoy in common but cannot purchase by themselves. Drawing here on the analysis of Inge Kaul and her colleagues at the United Nations Development Programme, it is evident that public goods once thought to be quintessentially domestic concerns (public health, prosperity-generating full employment, social peace) are better understood as global goods unattainable by any country alone.

Nor can the production or distribution of global public goods be left to that powerful engine of globalization, the market. Indeed, public goods share two characteristics that the market abhors. First, they can be enjoyed by any number of people simultaneously, so there is no price-deciding equilibrium of demand and supply. Second, it is difficult, even impossible, to

prevent someone from enjoying a public good once it exists —
even someone who doesn't pay for it. Investors cannot sequester
their own returns. A healthy ozone shield or stable capital markets
will benefit even those who contribute nothing to them.

If the market cannot deliver the goods, institutions must. But
today's institutions aren't. Kaul and others point to three
categories of failure:

- *A jurisdictional gap* — Policy issues are global, but policy-making
  is still primarily national in focus and reach.
- *A participation gap* — We live now in a multi-actor world. But,
  despite the pace of change, international cooperation is still
  too pre-eminently intergovernmental.
- *An incentive gap* — Cooperation works only if it promises a clear
  and fair deal to all parties, but today's cooperative attempts
  are often stymied in quarrels over distributions of costs
  and benefits.

These are failures of institutions and execution, process and
product. They are failures that jeopardize us all, and generations
to come. They cannot be overcome by any one country (at least,

not for long) except in concert with others. Equally, the global public goods we all need cannot be secured without being shared. They demand, and they promise, positive-sum bargains in which everybody stands to win.

In the following pages, we focus on three such global imperatives: preventing deadly conflict, meeting the needs of youth on a crowded planet, and managing climate change. Why these specific three? We chose them (from the numberless challenges the world now confronts) for completely pragmatic reasons. They are unambiguously important. They isolate, if only as examples, key global concerns in separate but interacting dimensions: peace and security, society and politics, economics and the environment. Each gives proof of calamitous failures in governance, and each points to ready remedies. Each invites discrete and practical actions by states and others in the global community. In sum, each of these three imperatives obliges states to govern collaboratively — or they will fail to govern at all.

PART 2

FOR THE MILLENNIUM ASSEMBLY: THREE IMPERATIVES OF GOVERNANCE

1. PREVENTING DEADLY CONFLICT

It is true to say, but only half-true, that most wars today are civil wars. They are fought against civilians for the most part, and it is mostly civilians who die. In cause and effect, however, it is truer to say that deadly conflict has been globalized. No war, no matter how local, can be fully understood (or prevented) without looking to the local impact of global markets, the global arms trade, the transborder loyalties of kinship and tradition, the fears and interests of other people and governments, and the growing influences of nonstate participants (whether mercenaries or Doctors Without Borders, Amnesty International or Alcoa). And just as television communicates the wickedness of war to a global audience, norms of human rights and good governance acquire a new and global authority.

No government, not even the most powerful, can any longer and by itself protect the security of its people. The only policy of national security is a policy of international security. Nor can any government defend the claim that whatever happens on its territory is nobody else's concern. That claim is denied by the UN Charter itself, and by an imposing number of treaties signed since (see Box 1). Deadly conflict, like the gross abuse of human rights that so often foretells conflict, has become everybody's business.

As the line between foreign and domestic begins to lose usefulness, so too do the old distinctions between intrastate war, interstate war, and the nonstate violence of terrorism. Insurgencies cross borders, as refugees do. Terrorists take the pay and protection of states. Government soldiers fight like criminals. Criminals do the dirty work of governments. To the innocent victims, the wrongs committed are practically indistinguishable. And to the world, they are just as menacing.

BOX 1

International Instruments for Human Rights

Twenty-five international instruments, adopted by the United Nations, protect and promote human rights around the world:

- Slavery Convention of 1926 (1926)
- Convention on the Prevention and Punishment of the Crime of Genocide (1948)
- Convention for the Suppression of the Traffic in Persons and of the Exploitation of the Prostitution of Others (1949)
- Convention Relating to the Status of Refugees (1951)
- Convention on the Political Rights of Women (1952)
- 1953 Protocol Amending the Slavery Convention of 1926 (1953)
- Slavery Convention of 1926 as amended (1953)
- Convention Relating to the Status of Stateless Persons (1954)
- Supplementary Convention on the Abolition of Slavery, the Slave Trade, and Institutions and Practices Similar to Slavery (1956)
- Convention on the Nationality of Married Women (1957)
- Convention on the Reduction of Statelessness (1961)
- Convention on the Consent to Marriage, Minimum Age for Marriage and Registration of Marriages (1962)
- International Convention on the Elimination of All Forms of Racial Discrimination (1965)
- International Covenant on Civil and Political Rights (1966)
- International Covenant on Economic, Social and Cultural Rights (1966)
- Optional Protocol to the International Covenant on Civil and Political Rights (1966)
- Protocol Relating to the Status of Refugees (1967)
- Convention on the Non-Applicability of Statutory Limitations to War Crimes and Crimes against Humanity (1968)
- International Convention on the Suppression and Punishment of the Crime of Apartheid (1973)
- Convention on the Elimination of All Forms of Discrimination against Women (1979)
- Convention against Torture and other Cruel, Inhuman or Degrading Treatment or Punishment (1984)
- International Convention against Apartheid in Sports (1985)
- Convention on the Rights of the Child (1989)
- Second Optional Protocol to the International Covenant on Civil and Political Rights (aims at the abolition of the death penalty) (1989)
- Convention on the Rights of Migrant Workers and the Members of their Families (1990)

If globalization tends to make conflict more lethal to more people in more countries, it also intensifies the urgency of prevention. And just as the causes and effects of deadly conflict are rarely contained in the territory of a single state, so must the prevention of conflict be a collaborative enterprise. Nobody can do it alone, but nobody can evade the obligation of doing it together.

Embedded though conflict usually is in the schisms and memories of conflict-prone societies, deadly conflict is not inevitable. On the contrary, war and other forms of organized violence usually follow considered decisions and intentional actions. Neither the genocide in Rwanda, nor the homicidal atrocities by government forces in Kosovo, nor the contemptible destruction in East Timor were spontaneous or natural or unavoidable. They were planned, decided, and done. Such things can be prevented.

But how? Lasting prevention means altering the conditions that give rise to violence. This is the long work of structural prevention: building peace by building good government, meeting basic human needs, and fostering social harmony. In this report, we focus on other measures: quickly achievable reforms of governance.

Plainly, existing institutions of governance have not adapted to the prevention of deadly conflict in the global age. The ghastly evidence lies all around us: in the graveyards of the Balkans, in the unspeakable wounds of children in Sierra Leone, in the narco-ruins of life in Colombia. In Cambodia, piles of skulls serve as war memorials. In Russia, Chechen lives have been blasted away and mothers weep at children's funerals.

Television, the Internet, the travels of relatives, the networks of NGOs — all serve to bring these conflicts home to us. They become, at least in some cases, our conflicts. And here globalization is having a powerful and complicating effect: globalized norms of human rights and democratic governance penetrate borders, reshaping old concepts of sovereignty and autonomy. People now see grotesque abuses of human rights on television; organize themselves in transborder NGOs; and experience and begin to understand linkages between corporate conduct, economic justice, individual security, democracy, and good government. A norm has formed and still develops – fitfully, with false starts and second thoughts – that legitimizes international intervention to stop the worst offences against human security and human rights. And, in the process, the meaning of national interest is being redefined. Sovereignty is rewired, and we see more clearly that what happens beyond our borders affects our own well-being and commands cooperative action.

The norm of intervention does not set up any absolute rule. It is one norm among many that guide the behaviour of governments and others in the global community. It coexists, restlessly and sometimes uneasily, with norms attached to sovereignty and the inviolability of borders. But nothing in the norms of sovereignty denies the reality of human rights, or the legitimacy of defending and restoring those rights.

As norms and rules are realigned to cope with new conditions, confusion reigns. But in all this uncertainty, the norm of intervention must not be traduced by the powerful (or the ambitious) as a pretext for interference in the affairs of the weak. As Algerian President Abdelaziz Bouteflika declared in the 1999 General Assembly: "Sovereignty is our final defence against the rules of an unequal world." This is a crucial element of the intervention norm: to have good and lasting effect, any act of intervention in the end must carry legitimacy. It is otherwise mere lawlessness. Small countries understand this acutely. So should any people whose prosperity and security are best served by maintaining an orderly peace in the world. Legitimacy is what the UN's authority pre-eminently provides to any exercise of military intervention.

In the worrying and commonly cited case of Kosovo, the NATO allies launched their bombardment of Yugoslavia without the authority of Security Council approval. Many have held, and argue still, that the NATO action was both illegal in international law and illegitimate. The US government and its allies answer that

the vicious abuses of life and liberty committed by the Milosevic regime justified the armed intervention (a lesser evil to stop the greater evil of ethnic cleansing, as it might be framed in just-war theory). What the NATO governments also emphasize is that the legitimizing approval of the Security Council was blocked by the (illegitimate?) threat of veto by Russia and China.

This makes a second point: just as an intervention decision must be legitimate to be fully effective, it must also be effective to be fully legitimate. When the Security Council declines to enforce its resolutions, or is indecisive, deadlocked by the veto, or careless of its obligations to peace and security, it will be condemned as ineffective by the rest of the world community. Similarly, it will be dismissed as ineffective when it refuses arbitrarily to intervene in some crises but intervenes in like crises elsewhere. When the Security Council lacks effectiveness, it loses legitimacy. The Kosovo case remains so disturbing because neither NATO's action nor the Security Council's inaction carried the legitimacy that intervention decisions require.

Early warning of deadly conflict is vital to effectiveness. The common and sinister sign of impending trouble is the abuse of human rights – committed by governments or tolerated by them (Box 2). Promptly detected, these are the wrongs that demand quick international action, before a larger tragedy follows.

But once the warning is heard, the effectiveness needs to be predictable. As Secretary-General Kofi Annan remarked in his 1999 annual report on the work of the UN: "Even the most repressive leaders watch to see what they can get away with. ... The more the international community succeeds in altering their destructive calculus, the more lives can be saved." A high level of certainty that the Security Council will intervene – with the durable international support that legitimacy provides – can deter some of the worst excesses of dictators and aggressors. For this reason, small countries vulnerable to various forms of mischief would benefit most from a stronger and more disciplined exercise of the norm of intervention, intervention that is both effective and legitimate.

This means that the global community cannot relegate the use of force to the option of last resort. Effective prevention, and particularly deterrence, require a readiness to use force when it will do the most good, not just when it is least inconvenient or politically inescapable. It is too soon for final judgments on the case of East Timor, but we venture this proposition: it is generally a mistake to try to decide a deep-seated dispute of this kind by referendum or plebiscite in the first instance. The very holding of the vote sets up a zero-sum confrontation between total loss and total victory, inciting violence from those who expect to lose. Better to create conditions of at least minimal security (and even, with good fortune, a civil dialogue) and later – in relative serenity, with power-sharing and other formulations to ponder – arrange an election on the future. In such cases, an armed international presence should be one of the first resorts, not the last, to prevent conflict and advance a democratic settlement. In East Timor, had Indonesian authorities permitted it, tragedy might have been prevented by a sufficient deployment of force earlier rather than later in the ballot process.

Just as early warning is crucial to prevention and successful intervention, so is careful and patient follow-up. This is not to argue that every mission needs a precisely scheduled exit strategy (even if that's what generals want). What is always necessary, however, is an agreed understanding of realizable objectives and a shared determination to achieve them. That will include preparation of the critical transition from military to civilian administration in most cases, and investments in subsequent political and economic development. These are long-term (and sometimes costly) commitments, typically hard to negotiate. But interventions lacking these undertakings will very likely lack both effectiveness and legitimacy.

In the Security Council itself, the effectiveness and legitimacy of its proceedings would be immeasurably enhanced by a curtailment of the veto and expansion of membership. We propose neither here. Such reforms mean changing the Charter. There is no consensus on such amendments and regrettably little will to create a consensus.

Still the facts remain. Overuse of the veto robs the Council and its permanent members of both effectiveness and legitimacy. And as for the Council's anachronistic membership, it is an injustice and an impediment to success. It does not represent the people of the world, or even the current politics of interstate relations. There has developed, moreover, a malign interaction of veto and inequitable membership, in the form of secret meetings of the Permanent Five from which the other ten Council members are methodically excluded. Again, effectiveness and legitimacy are lost, and the incongruity of membership and procedures grows more destabilizing by the day.

Speaking of lost legitimacy, it is impossible not to be reminded that the largest dealers in the global arms market every year include the Council's Permanent Five: Britain, China, France, Russia, and the United States. Those governments ought to be asked more often how they reconcile peace, security, and human well-being with selling death.

Meanwhile, however, reform can occur without Charter amendments. The Secretary-General, the Assembly, and the Council have already made praiseworthy progress; much more is possible. Abuse of the veto, for instance, could be usefully reduced by an informal but explicit agreement among the Permanent Five on three simple rules. First, each of the Five should declare as policy that it will not impose or threaten a

veto on any question that is purely procedural. Second, on substantive questions, each should declare that it will apply its veto only against resolutions directly and significantly threatening its own vital interests. And third, every exercise of the veto should be accompanied by a (convincing) public statement to justify it. Such a three-part reform is not far-fetched. In truth, the United States for many years forswore its use of the veto unilaterally. It might productively do so again: a self-imposed commitment to our three suggested rules will tend to encourage or embarrass others to announce likewise. At a stroke, it would also regain for the US government a standing in the UN corresponding more closely to its standing in the world. (Although its reputation will never fully recover, nor should it, until the United States reliably pays its UN debts in full and without conditions.) Below, we propose six more recommendations for the better prevention of deadly conflict.

When the Secretary-General finds after an investigation
that serious human-rights abuses are or may be occurring,
to which the Security Council is not already responding,
he should refer his finding to the General Assembly.
We believe that if a sizeable and representative Assembly majority
concluded in a resolution that such violations were taking place,
it would prove much harder politically for a permanent Council
member to veto remedial action. The Assembly's freedom to act
in such cases is constrained only by the Charter's prohibition (in
Article 12) against the Assembly making a "recommendation" in
respect of an issue on which the Council is already "exercising ...
the functions assigned to it" by the Charter. In short, the
Assembly is entitled to address a problem that the Council is
avoiding. And it should be recalled that the Assembly in the past
has acted resolutely in such matters; among other operations,
the United Nations Emergency Force in 1956 (the first true
peacekeeping deployment to the Middle East) was established
by the Assembly. Without changing the Charter, the Assembly
could change the politics of Security Council decision-making,
rendering the veto far less easy to threaten or deploy without
persuasive justification.

The Secretary-General, with others, should strengthen
the apparatus of conflict warning.
Violations of human rights — themselves often violent —
commonly precede deadly conflict. They can give early warning,
and time for prevention. The Secretary-General has tightened
and streamlined coordination among UN agencies in the field
and at headquarters. Those efforts, and outreach to NGO,
business, and academic communities, should be systematically
intensified. NGOs and UN agencies are frequently the first
to witness the injustices and imminent dangers that abuses
represent. And after conflict does erupt, they can supply valuable
intelligence to guide helpful intervention, whether as aid or
sanctions, diplomacy or armed force. To the same end, the

Secretary-General should activate more frequently Article 99
of the Charter — the open authority of his office to "bring to
the attention of the Security Council any matter which in his
opinion may threaten the maintenance of international peace
and security."

To enhance the Secretary-General's capacity to detect and
resolve incipient crises, UN member states should contribute
significantly to the Fund for Preventive Action.
The Fund, established by Norway in 1996, can become an
important resource for the Secretary-General to train, support,
and expand a roster of people to serve as envoys and special
representatives in real or apprehended crises. It is a familiar but
easily neglected fact that quiet diplomacy, well timed, can prevent
deadly conflict or its spread. It is money well spent, but it is
money that member states spend too little of. In every case,
early prevention is far cheaper than the cost of later armed
intervention and postconflict reconstruction.

The Secretary-General and Security Council must have more capacity for rapid reaction to imminent conflict.
The carnage in East Timor, much of which occurred while the Council and member states laboriously assembled an intervention force, demonstrated again the necessity of timely deployment. Various member governments have made useful proposals for rapid-reaction and standby forces on call for UN duty. Existing primitive arrangements need improving. The designation of rapid-reaction forces by member states would hasten deployments by "coalitions of the willing" in emergencies (and reduce reliance on superpower contributions). It would also facilitate participation in UN-authorized missions by smaller and middle powers otherwise unable to field large forces at short notice. Capacity would be further enhanced by the creation of a small standing police force, at the call of the Secretary-General and the Council. Police are invariably harder to get from member states even than troops (because police are never in over-supply domestically); yet the inexpensive deployment of police on short notice can subdue an imminent crisis and bring a reassuring peace to the aftermath.

Far more political and organizational energy must be invested in the safe management, and reduction, of nuclear arsenals.
Any use of nuclear weapons would be catastrophic. For exactly that reason, nuclear weapons are militarily useless as instruments of state power. They remain, however, a menace to the world, not least as weapons of terror. Which is why, given the sorry improbability of early and complete nuclear disarmament, there is an urgent need for a better accounting of weapons and materials, with a closer monitoring of their whereabouts and condition. The real and immediate problems are these: to re-establish dependable control over the former Soviet warheads; to reduce the numbers of Russian and US warhead-delivery vehicles; to take more nuclear forces off alert; to explore the stabilizing effects of reciprocal no-first-use commitments; and to prevent proliferation to potential rogue states and others. Yet the various regimes intended to limit the proliferation of weapons of mass destruction, and discourage their use, have fallen into an alarming disarray. The US Senate's

repudiation of the Comprehensive Test Ban Treaty, and the unsettling prospect that the United States will try to deploy missile-defence systems, only aggravate the dangers of future weapons races and a new proliferation.

Even now, despite the initiatives of nuclear arms reduction already completed, an appalling number of warheads remain around the world – a condition made more dangerous by the deplorable activities of India and Pakistan. To believe so many weapons can be kept indefinitely and never used is fanciful optimism. The risks of inadvertence, misperception, miscalculation, terrorism, or madness – and the apocalyptic consequences – are too great to tolerate.

The culture of prevention must be fostered.
The UN in its many forums, led by the Secretary-General, is well placed to instill attitudes and skills of conflict prevention precisely because the organization is (putting it delicately) organized flexibly. In its many disparate parts, responding in many ways to many problems, the UN can foster networks of diverse disciplines, professions, and experiences to chart promising courses of peaceful and sustainable development. The Secretary-General

and his team have striven to manage these agency activities more coherently, assembling new and stronger coalitions to address key issues. More can be done by way of staffing and training within the UN, particularly in exploiting the contributions that development can make to conflict prevention. The UN can also sponsor assemblies of political, business, and NGO leaders to explore what divides these constituencies, and what brings them together. And it can invite business leaders to share more systematically their particular insights into political and economic obstacles to development. To repeat: deadly conflicts, and the conflictful elements of globalization, are usually not inevitable or irresistible. They are more often, and in large part, outcomes of decisions. Institutionalizing better decisions, the better to prevent deadly conflict, is the challenge of good governance.

2. PROVIDING OPPORTUNITIES FOR THE YOUNG

The planet's human population has now surpassed six billion. Some one billion of us are teenagers, a fact with two inescapable consequences. First, nature being what it is, this cohort of one billion will very soon begin to produce tens of millions of new babies of their own every year. Second, and in the meantime, we will all experience the energetic clamour of a billion adolescents transforming our cultures, economies, and politics. Nothing will affect human well-being more certainly than the actions we take now to provide for these new and future generations of young people.

Demography is not destiny, but it counts for something. The human population, now expanding by about 80 million people a year, is generally projected to reach about eight billion in 2025. (It was 1.65 billion in 1900.) True, fertility rates have fallen globally and rates of population increases have subsided. But with a huge generation of females just entering their childbearing years, the experts foresee a global population that continues to grow well beyond 2025. (At the same time, to confuse things, the number of people older than 60 is projected to double in 25 years, to 1.2 billion; in some rich countries, supporting the elderly is a challenge to governance as daunting as providing for the young.)

About 98 percent of global population growth will occur in the poorer countries of the South, where 80 percent of people now live (and where two billion are classified as malnourished). As well, by 2025 the number of people living in urban areas will reach five billion – twice the urban population of 1990. By way of contrast, in 1950 New York and London were the only two megacities of at least eight million people; by 1995, 23 cities had surpassed eight million, 17 of them in developing countries (Table 1). By 2015, the UN Population Division expects there will be 36 such megacities, 23 of them in Asia.

These are intimidating numbers, but they don't capture the scale of the coming crisis for young people, or for the rest of us. The calamity is in the context: inequalities of income and opportunity that grow worse and not better; absolute deprivation that intensifies for millions; environmental exhaustion; bloody struggles of scarcity, living space, and systems of belief; and lethal failures of governance.

TABLE 1
Expected Growth in Cities with Populations
of 8 Million or More.

Megacity	Population (millions)	
	1995	2015
Tokyo, Japan	26.96	28.89
Mexico City, Mexico	16.56	19.18
São Paulo, Brazil	16.53	20.32
New York, USA	16.33	17.60
Bombay, India*	15.14	26.22
Shanghai, China	13.58	17.97
Los Angeles, USA	12.41	14.22
Calcutta, India	11.92	17.31
Buenos Aires, Argentina	11.80	13.86
Seoul, South Korea	11.61	12.98
Beijing, China	11.30	15.57
Osaka, Japan	10.61	10.61
Lagos, Nigeria*	10.29	24.61
Rio de Janeiro, Brazil	10.18	11.86
Delhi, India*	9.95	16.86
Karachi, Pakistan*	9.73	19.38
Cairo, Egypt	9.69	14.42
Paris, France	9.52	9.69
Tianjin, China	9.42	13.53
Metro Manila, Philippines*	9.29	14.66
Moscow, Russia	9.27	9.30
Jakarta, Indonesia*	8.62	13.92
Dhaka, Bangladesh*	8.55	19.49

* Cities expected to grow by more that 50 percent by 2015.

UNICEF, in *The Progress of Nations 1999*, pictured the birth of a child in the century's last months, the six-billionth baby in a population of six billion, and drew the face of inequality. That child had less than 1 chance in 10 of being born into relative prosperity, and 3 chances in 10 of suffering extreme poverty. (At last estimate, more than 1.2 billion human beings are straining to survive on incomes of US $1 or less a day.) Born in Malawi or Uganda, that child will probably live half as long as one born the same day in Singapore or Sweden. The child might well be already an orphan; every year, 600 000 women die from pregnancy-related causes or in childbirth, nearly all of them in developing countries. Millions more children have been orphaned by AIDS. For want of education and health care, the six-billionth child will suffer even greater hardships if she is a girl.

The effects of these disparities on the young are manifold and dangerous. They imperil social peace, exclude millions from a share of globalization's benefits, and foreclose opportunities for future development. It is in these inequalities that we see the intricate connections between development and freedom. Poverty imprisons the poor; that much is well understood. But the wealthy in divided societies — cringing in their armed and gated compounds, afraid of the night and the future — can hardly be described as free. Inequalities have a way of claiming everyone as victims.

And the global disparities are plentiful. Thailand has more cell phones than all of Africa. As for the Internet, North America with 5 percent of the world's population accounts for almost 50 percent of all Internet users. UNDP makes the reinforcing point that income buys access, and thus the chance for more income. Buying a computer would cost the average Bangladeshi more than 8 years' income, compared with 1 month's for an average American.

Furthermore, there is a pernicious synergy to globalization that sooner or later seems to entangle every problem in every other problem. Resource scarcity drives poor people to over-use soils or forests, causing more poverty; ethnic conflict motivates migration, squeezing strangers together, disrupting economies, and igniting new conflict; malevolent government leads to violence, displacement, and poverty, and then (often) more malevolent government.

It is probable, for example, that by 2025 two of every three people in the world will have to live with water scarcities of some degree — and with all the potential for dispute and conflict that such scarcities imply. But scarcities alone don't cause conflict or chronic poverty. Rather, scarcities combine explosively with other political, economic, and cultural factors in chain reactions of privation, grievance, war, and migration. These are the borderless interactions that threaten us all, and especially the young. They reconstruct our ideas of sovereignty and space, and reorganize our national interests. And they will demand good governance, within and across national borders.

No interaction of globalization endangers the young more surely than the sovereign debt that poor countries owe to the rich (Box 3). Indeed, UNDP has reported that debt servicing has exceeded health spending in 29 heavily indebted poor countries, including 23 in sub-Saharan Africa. At the same time, of course, global flows of official development aid have declined throughout the 1990s, while debt charges have risen. The costs to children, in the present and into the future, continue to mount.

The slow-moving program of debt relief for these countries, insufficiently strengthened in 1999, therefore needs radical acceleration along the practical lines proposed by UNDP, Oxfam, Jubilee 2000, and several creditor countries. Moreover, debt relief should be linked explicitly to added investments in constructive development: education, health, environmental protection, and the like. Here we are only reasserting what everyone knows: these debts are an insupportable burden on poor economies; they are unpayable and uncollectable. The children meanwhile suffer.

BOX 3

Children Pay the Price

Debt has a child's face. Debt's burden falls most heavily on the minds and bodies of children, killing some, and stunting others so that they will never fully develop. It leaves children without immunization against fatal, but easily preventable, diseases. It condemns them to a life without education or — if they go to school — to classrooms without roofs, desks, chairs, blackboards, books, even pencils. And it orphans them, as hundreds of thousands of mothers die in childbirth each year, die as a result of inadequacies in health care and other services that poverty perpetuates.

Certainly, developing country governments that favour their own elites over their poor also bear much of the responsibility. But debt's demands make it hard for many governments to restructure their budgets towards more child-centred priorities even when they want to, and make it well-nigh impossible to succeed even if they do. Sub-Saharan Africa, for example, spends more on servicing its $200 billion debt than on the health and education of its 306 million children. The pattern is economically senseless and morally indefensible.

— *Shridath Ramphal*

Persisting inequalities, a more squalid poverty in the teeming new megacities, environmental destruction as millions more people deplete the land for food and fuel, a rising probability of conflict: these are the terrible implications of misgovernance, embedded in a shared failure to provide for our children and their children. But failure is not inevitable. There are preventive remedies at hand that are practical, affordable, and effective. They are not available to any government acting alone. They require the collaboration of governments with others in the global community, and a modest commitment of political courage. Here the UN can claim ready-made advantages in its infrastructure of institutions, expertise, and processes. This is where the unique character of the UN — its universality, its power to convoke, its particular legitimacy — creates real openings for leadership and action.

To prove the possibility of cooperative action, here are four pragmatic endeavours that can dramatically open opportunities for youth by enhancing their access to the necessities of life.

Rescue the children from the HIV/AIDS plague.
More than 33 million people in the world are now living with HIV and AIDS. Over 14 million have already died – more than 11 million of them in Africa, where AIDS leads all other causes of death in the 15–24 age group. By the end of 2000, 13 million or more of the world's children will have lost their mothers or both parents to AIDS.

Ninety percent of new infections occur in poor countries, disproportionately in Africa. Two million Africans were killed by AIDS in 1998, 10 times more than in all the continent's wars that year. Women and children suffer especially. In sub-Saharan Africa, six adolescent girls are infected for every boy the same age – the misogynistic arithmetic of male promiscuity and female powerlessness. As a result, HIV infection rates among pregnant women in Africa are fearfully high: at least 20 percent in many countries, as high as 60 percent in some towns. Children die of AIDS because they become infected or because their families are impoverished by its effects. Orphaned or not, they are victims in the end of malnutrition, inadequate health care, prejudice, and neglect.

This is a global plague. (India now counts more people living with HIV and AIDS than any other country.) It demands a global response, for the children's sake.

A public-private partnership, with the personal encouragement of the UN Secretary-General, has reached an early stage of formation for the purpose of combating HIV and AIDS in Africa. We urge prompt progress in that project, with the objective of cutting HIV infection rates among the young by 25 percent in 5 years. That requires an energetic collaboration of UN agencies, African and industrialized-country governments, and the private sector. Prevention is key to achieving the goal, through education, counselling, and frank public debate. But success almost certainly demands something else: an improved access to expensive drugs in countries too poor to buy them at current prices. This might mean relaxing patent protections — and trade rules — that keep those drug prices unaffordably high. Here again, a transborder threat demands a cooperative response. The governance challenge is to reward invention while properly distributing invention's benefits.

Enrol every child in basic education.
Through all of the 1990s, and with disheartening frequency, delegations at international conferences have solemnly accepted the obligation of universal access to primary education — and just as frequently failed to honour it. This is profoundly destructive, condemning millions of young people to a future barren of opportunity or hope. In *The State of the World's Children 2000*, UNICEF estimates that more than 130 million children worldwide are not in school. Worse, millions more children work in hazardous or unhealthy labour instead of going to school. Basic education, formal or informal, in class or not, can rescue whole communities for a better future. More than half the

children who are not in school are girls. This is an injustice, and a waste. To quote *The Progress of Nations 1999*: "As more girls are educated, and for longer periods, their confidence and empowerment will rise, and infant mortality and population growth will fall – all of this a boon to life expectancy and overall economic growth."

Big capital projects are not the measure of success here; the object is to educate, not to build schools. And there are successful models to learn from. In Brazil, for example, the *Comunidade Solidária* programs train thousands of young people every year for productive employment. In several Asian countries, the International Youth Foundation has started a program in which multinational firms finance training in community development for young female factory workers, to use when they return to their villages for marriage. Modest in their way, these efforts demonstrate the barely explored value available in government–business–NGO partnerships.

This is a classic case of quite minuscule investments yielding tremendous returns. Small diversions of national budgets and aid allocations to basic education, in close cooperation with NGOs,

international organizations, and others, will generate literally life-changing improvements. Why is such easy action so scarce? The shamefully obvious explanation is that children are politically weak. They can neither threaten nor promise, and they have no vote. But when the trifling cost is measured against the huge and lasting benefits, government leaders have no excuse not to act; they still have their own promises to keep.

Expand access to the Internet in developing countries, especially for the young.
Access to telecommunications (and, in a real sense, to the future) is constricted by geography, gender, income, and language. In fact, half of humankind has never placed a phone call. Modest investments, and the removal of obstructing government regulations, can enable more people to access the World Wide Web, dial a cell phone, or to use satellite TV for something more than ESPN. From Estonia to India, town halls and village schools are going online (Estonia has more computers per capita than France or Italy). Inexpensive, fast, and accessible communications free people and their organizations to learn about agronomy, the treatment of diarrhea, or the redress of a human-rights violation. Now, with satellite and cellular systems, poor economies can skip the old pole-and-wire technologies altogether as they sign on to the communications revolution. And the Internet is startlingly cheap, as UNDP has noted: to send a 40-page document from Madagascar to Côte d'Ivoire can cost $75 by 5-day courier, $45 for a 30-minute fax, or less than 20 cents by 2-minute email.

But the Internet so far has polarized the world in yet another inequality of haves and have-nots, the plugged-in and the unplugged. South Asia is home to 20 percent of the global population, but less than 1 percent of Internet users. Even with the new technologies, installation costs are significant where (as in much of rural Africa) telephone services are scarce. And, of course, Internet connections hardly benefit the illiterate and the innumerate.

This is why policies for basic education, economic development, and communications regulation are all of a piece in the present age – and why governments must collaborate with NGOs, industry, and international organizations to share the gains of globalization. In the Philippines and Senegal, to cite two good examples, telephone companies were required to provide specified services to rural and poor communities as a condition of their licences. In Bangladesh and Mauritius, governments eliminated tariffs and taxes on personal computers to foster their proliferation. These are manageable reforms at small cost, for large returns, if they are enforced.

It should also be said that faster, cheaper global communications will make people more aware of their own government's performance in comparison with the (now visible) performance of others, and maybe less tolerant of failures. This is not a bad thing, if good governance is an objective.

Two more actions to protect children's health
(and redeem a few other broken promises).
The links between wealth and health are hard and unforgiving.
Children in poverty are commonly denied basic health care,
schooling, safe water, and sanitation. If they survive, they grow up
and die poor. The diseases of poverty prey with special tragedy on
the young. Malaria, for example, claims as many as three million
lives every year, 80 percent of them children. With up to half a
million new cases occurring a year, the incidence of this disease,
once assumed eradicable, is actually rising around the world.
Malaria is one of the many preventable diseases that thrive
in poverty.

In point of fact, the best that could be done for the health of the
world's children (including those in rich countries) would be to
raise the incomes of the poor. But we do not plead here for some
grand new design to eliminate poverty. Instead, we remind
governments of their own (unkept) promises of the 1990 World
Summit for Children – and advance two modest proposals.

First: Discourage tobacco consumption.
In the words of Gro Harlem Brundtland, Director-General of
the World Health Organization: "Wherever we come from and
whatever we do, we are never truly safe from the long arm of the
tobacco industry as they search the world for new markets and
victims." But because per-capita cigarette consumption is
generally declining in the rich countries, tobacco companies
are creating those new markets – and new victims – mostly in
middle-income and developing economies. The exposure of the
young to tobacco smoke, and their early addiction to nicotine,
together represent one of the great and ominous public-health
menaces of this new century.

Already, about four million people a year die of smoking-
related illnesses: 11 000 preventable deaths a day. WHO estimates
10 million a year will be dying from smoking by about 2025,

70 percent of them in developing countries. Meantime, the number of smokers globally is expected on current trends to rise to 1.6 billion in 2025 from the present 1.1 billion. Since there is a lag of 25 to 30 years between the onset of chronic smoking and death, the future's casualty rates are built into today's addiction rates.

Children are victimized twice: first as the offspring of smoking parents, then as smokers themselves. Children of smoking mothers suffer higher rates of intrauterine retardation and low birthweight. Evidence indicates that having a parent who smokes increases risks of sudden infant death syndrome, respiratory illnesses, ear infections, learning difficulties, and language impairment. Then, in their teens or sooner, the young are the vulnerable targets of tobacco industry marketing – on television and movie screens and billboards, in discos and stadiums, in magazines – all identifying cigarette smoking with what is glamorous, successful, sexy, and worldly. To quote Brundtland again: "It is rare – if not impossible – to find examples in history that match tobacco's programmed trail of death and destruction."

Policies to stop smoking can succeed; they are succeeding now in many countries, if not fast or thoroughly enough. But they can only ultimately prevail if pursued globally, as a collaboration of governments, business, science, NGOs, and international institutions, with marketing programs as sophisticated as tobacco's own. A good start was made in 1999, with the launch of the WHO-sponsored Framework Convention on Tobacco Control. The Convention rightly reflects the fact that suppressing tobacco consumption must be multisectoral: tax increases (especially effective in discouraging the young from buying their first smokes); agricultural transition programs; "counter-advertising" against the industry and its products; prohibitions on sales to minors and against smoking in the workplace and public places; warning labels; strict controls on tobacco advertising and promotions; and transnational action against smuggling. We recommend adoption of the Convention by May 2003, as WHO proposes. The pay-off for reducing cigarette smoking is prompt and lasting, in higher tax revenues, lower health-care costs, and smaller losses in productivity. The suffering thereby prevented is incalculable.

Second: Get the lead out.

The health and futures of children everywhere can be quickly and markedly improved by removing lead from gasoline. Lead is a poisonous heavy metal, especially toxic to the brain, kidneys, the reproductive system, and cardiovascular function. As the World Resources Institute and others have reported, lead poisoning remains the single most significant and preventable disease associated with an environmental toxin. And it is a special hazard to young children: lead exposures reduce children's IQs and are linked to attention disorders, aggression, and delinquency.

Leaded gasoline is by far the largest source of lead exposure in urban areas: about 90 percent of all lead emissions in the air come from gasoline. Aside from posing an immediate health risk when inhaled, lead accumulates in soils, drinking water, and in the food chain.

Despite all this hard evidence, however, scarcely more than a dozen countries have phased out leaded gasoline (Figure 2). This represents both an opportunity and an obligation. Lead poisoning can be prevented easily and cheaply. With available technology and in short order, the lives and life chances of millions of children would be immediately enhanced by an internationally coordinated program of removing lead from gasoline. Experience in Mexico City and the United States, for example, shows blood lead levels decline almost instantaneously as lead emissions fall (Figure 3).

FIGURE 2

Use of Leaded Gasoline Worldwide.

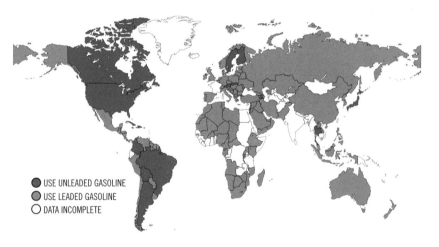

What can achieve such a success? Public education can teach consumers the virtues of unleaded fuels and build public support for policy changes. And market-based incentives can lubricate refinery conversion. For example, during a (quite brief) phase-out period, fuel taxes can help to price leaded gasoline higher than unleaded. In Britain, according to the World Resources Institute, the price differential between leaded and unleaded petrol has grown to 11 percent as consumers and vehicle manufacturers complete the transition.

Facilitated through existing UN networks and agencies, a lead-abolition campaign would do more than improve the health of children. It would create new practices and associations among governments, businesses, and institutions — groundwork for future cooperation in pollution abatement, energy conservation, or the management of climate change. Good governance begets better governance.

There is an additional happy bonus to lead-removal programs: countries can recover the costs, 5 or 10 times over, in lower health-care costs, savings on engine maintenance, and longer engine life. This is why government–industry–public collaboration can be so profitable. The health and economic pay-offs are rich enough to reward all participants in the program. And the first to benefit are children.

FIGURE 3

Decreases in Blood Lead Values and Amounts of Lead Used in Gasoline in the United States, 1976–1980.

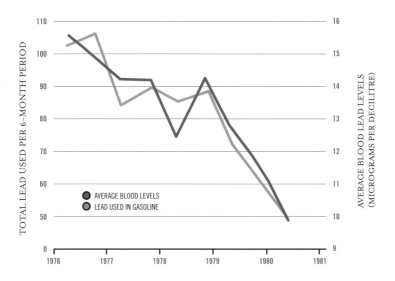

3. MANAGING CLIMATE CHANGE

This we know. The Arctic ice is melting. Global mean sea levels have risen 10 to 15 centimetres in the past century. Sea levels have reached their highest in 5 000 years, and are rising now at a rate 10 times faster than the average during that period. The 1990s were the hottest decade since measurements started in the 1860s; 1998 was hotter than any year before. Surface air temperatures around the world are higher now than a century ago (Figure 4). Earth's climate is changing.

FIGURE 4
Surface Air Temperature from 1860 to 1997.

We also know, with a grim and growing certainty, that some part at least of global warming is human-made. This is not the first period of climate change in the history of the planet. But there is now a formidable and strengthening consensus among scientists, and an increasing consistency of evidence, on the links between the production of greenhouse gases and the warming of the atmosphere. (The World Meteorological Organization reckons, from the evidence of tree rings, ice cores, and other data, that the

20th century was the hottest in a thousand years.) Science tells us that, up to a point, the greenhouse effect is both natural and necessary. Greenhouse gases (chiefly carbon dioxide, CO_2) allow sunlight to reach the Earth's surface, then block infrared radiation bouncing back into space; that's what keeps us warm. Too much of those greenhouse gases, however, will keep us too warm. And since the start of the industrial revolution, the cumulative tonnages of CO_2 emissions into the atmosphere have increased a thousandfold, mostly from burning fossil fuels.

The climate warming already measured closely follows computer-model projections of what human-made greenhouse gases would do to atmospheric temperatures. By 1996, the Inter-Governmental Panel on Climate Change had concluded that there is "a discernible human influence on global climate." Harder to predict – and even more troubling – are the coming consequences of global warming. (Not only was 1998 the hottest year yet, it was also the worst year ever recorded for weather-related disasters. Floods and storms killed tens of thousands of people and displaced millions from their homes and livelihoods.) Climatologists expect the energy stored in a warmer atmosphere will generate stronger storms and ocean surges. Thawing icecaps will raise sea levels, threatening coastal areas and island states with inundation. Rainfall could increase significantly in some regions, while droughts descend on others. Biodiversity could be lost as species fail to adapt fast enough to their altered environments. Tropical diseases like malaria and dengue would likely migrate north and south.

As the United Nations Environment Programme has glumly reported in its *Outlook 2000*, global warming "now seems inevitable." Even allowing for possible benign effects (longer growing seasons at higher latitudes?), simple prudence argues for action against the real and multiple dangers. One class of precaution will have to include measures to cope with effects already under way: protection or even evacuation of vulnerable coastal populations (Figure 5); reforestation against hillside erosion and desertification; breeding new crops to thrive in different weather; immunization and other public health

FIGURE 5
Heavily Populated Delta Regions that Are
Vulnerable to Sea Level Rise.

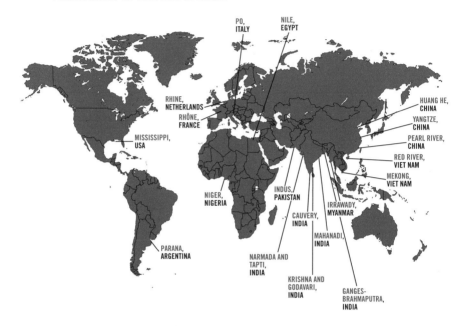

programs. Note well: phenomena like coastal flooding, the
intensification of storms, and the destabilizing thaw of northern
tundra are part of the warming that has already occurred.
Inaction is not an option, and indifference will lead to
greater disaster.

Just as urgent are the longer-term actions that prudence requires
to suppress future greenhouse-gas emissions (and brake the speed
of future warming). Some of the challenges here are technical;
those are the easy ones. The hard problems are political and
institutional, problems of governance. The technical issues have
to do with engineering and cost recovery. The politics are all
about who pays, and who benefits.

The problem of effectively managing climate change gives proof
of how unprepared we are with institutions to secure global public
goods. The problem is global, but policy-making is still mostly
national. The problem can only be solved by networks of firms,
scientists, engineers, producers, and consumers, but our
institutions and negotiations are still mostly intergovernmental.
And while everybody stands to gain by minimizing the global
harm of climate change, the actual gains and costs can bear
unequally and unfairly on people around the world.

Let us say (as the scientific consensus does) that global CO_2
emissions must be cut below 1990 levels just to stabilize future
atmospheric concentrations even at higher levels. Who in the
world should do the cutting? Rich industrial countries — the
ones that mostly got us into this mess? Or developing countries —
whose energy demands and carbon emissions are rising fastest?
And, to ask the more basic question, how should that issue be
decided?

What we cannot do is shirk these questions. Global energy use, as
reported by the World Resources Institute, has increased almost
70 percent since 1971; it is projected to rise more than 2 percent
annually for the next 15 years. Without concerted international
action, that alone would raise greenhouse-gas emissions about
50 percent higher than current levels. Without intervention,
the rate of global warming will accelerate, and so will the
accumulation of risks. Sovereignty, in these circumstances, will
only have meaning in global collaboration, and the interests
of states are bound inextricably to the interests of others.

So we are back to governance, to politics and institutions.
Suppressing greenhouse-gas emissions demands thoroughgoing
economic transformation — starting with reductions in the burning
of coal and oil, the high-carbon fossil fuels that do much of the
damage. That means new kinds of engines, whole new systems of

transportation, new buildings and new industrial processes. It can also mean the destruction of entire industries, and the collapse of the communities they support. Again, who pays?

The answer can begin with a cheerful array of truths. In the first place, the speed of global economic change itself can absorb much of the shock. The World Bank has estimated that as much as 80 percent of world industrial output in 2010 will be produced by firms that today do not even exist; those firms will be born into a low-carbon global economy, if that is what we decide to create. In the second place, new fortunes will be made and benefits derived from the clean new industries that will overtake or resupply dirty old industries — if markets are properly organized. (Somebody will have to build the motors that replace gasoline engines, and sell natural-gas burners for power plants.) In the third place, the same (expensive) measures that can reduce the rise in CO_2 emissions in the long run can yield welcome side-effects in the short run, including air-quality improvements saving hundreds of thousands of lives every year.

For all the money that governments and others will have to spend to manage climate change, there is much money to be saved as well (Table 2). Think what governments everywhere spend on subsidies for energy, agriculture, roads, and water consumption — all factors in the environmentally harmful, high-carbon economy. As an Earth Council report has observed, the world is "spending hundreds of billions of dollars annually to support its own destruction." By eliminating such subsidies and redistributing the proceeds, governments can save money while they save the Earth.

So there is a general global interest in controlling global warming's worst effects, and particular costs to be paid. To distribute those costs and benefits fairly and effectively, what is needed is a "grand bargain" and the governance to keep it. To that end, we offer here four practical approaches.

TABLE 2

The World's 10 Most Costly Insurance Losses.

Event	Year	Loss (billions of US $)
Hurricane Andrew (USA)	1992	18.0
Northridge earthquake (USA)	1994	13.5
Hurricane Mireille (Japan)	1991	6.5
Winter storm Daria (Europe)	1990	5.6
Hurricane Hugo (Puerto Rico)	1989	5.4
Autumn storm (Europe)	1987	4.2
Winter storm Vivian (Europe)	1990	3.9
Piper Alpha explosion (Britian)	1988	2.7
Kobe earthquake (Japan)	1995	2.6
Hurricane Opal (USA)	1995	2.2

Breathe new political life into the Kyoto Protocol.

More than 170 governments have ratified the 1992 Framework
Convention on Climate Change, agreed at the Rio Earth Summit.
That committed industrialized countries to negotiate the
restoration of greenhouse-gas emissions by 2000 to the levels of
1990, an undertaking they now cannot meet. The 1997 Kyoto
Protocol to the Convention commits industrialized countries to
cut emissions of six greenhouse gases by at least 5 percent from
1990 levels by 2012. This would only be a small step toward the
declared aim of stabilizing accumulations of greenhouse gases in
the atmosphere. But it is a step not yet taken.

The Kyoto Protocol represents more than a life-saving but
unfulfilled commitment. It also provides the rudimentary but
useful outline of the essential grand bargain between rich and
developing countries. The Convention and Protocol together
suggest the sequence and character of cooperative actions that rich
and poor countries must take if the planet we all inhabit is to be
rescued from the worst effects of global warming. In short, rich

countries can meet their Kyoto commitments both by investing in emission reductions at home and by transferring money and technology to poor countries. Either way, an industrialized country earns emission credits that can be applied to its own account or traded internationally. The bargain turns on the pivotal fact that a dollar spent by a rich country in a poor country can generate a more powerful climate-saving benefit than a dollar spent domestically. The governance challenge is to organize that mutually beneficial transaction, in a coordination of governments, industries, and communities.

Accelerate the start-up of the Clean Development Mechanism.

The Clean Development Mechanism (CDM) is a key governance innovation contained in the Kyoto Protocol, but so far remains little more than words on paper. Significantly, many of the governments that signed the Protocol have been slower to act than firms around the world that are already creating a market in emission-reduction programs – political decision again falling behind business innovation. The CDM is the machinery that can put the bargain in motion, helping industrialized countries meet

their emission obligations at home while helping to finance a rising prosperity in the poor countries. The CDM can, and should, become a critical instrument of sustainable development.

For example (and hypothetically), the European Union and Nigeria might conclude that a million dollars invested in Nigeria on clean-power generation and oilfield improvements would yield far greater emission reductions than a million dollars spent in Europe. Mediated through the CDM with active industry involvement, the EU transfer of money and technology would count as a contribution to Europe's emission-reduction commitment and speed Nigerian development. Or, Japan and Brazil might calculate that Amazon reforestation and restoration — recreating the natural "carbon sink" that absorbs CO_2 from the atmosphere — would cost less than a comparable reduction of emissions in Japan. Forest conservation (with its many other benefits) could count toward Japan's Kyoto obligation.

The CDM has been too slow to move, partly because of the details and partly because too few governments have deployed sufficient will. (Progress has also been impeded because authority and obligation have been spread too thinly across several UN institutions.) One answer is to start bilaterally instead of multilaterally, with demonstration projects showing how emissions trading might work. Prototypes already present themselves. In Costa Rica, the Netherlands and Sweden have bought developing-country debt in exchange for reforestation; in effect, the three countries together are converting a financial obligation into a global public good. Canada and Honduras have struck a similar bargain. Swapping debt for greenhouse-gas action looks entirely doable, and productive.

The CDM lacks an institutional platform. Build one. UNDP and others have suggested an "international bank for environmental settlements." As described in UNDP's 1998 *Human Development Report*, the bank "would act as a clearing house for the global environmental market, matching parties in environmental trade, mediating borrowing and lending and ensuring the integrity of market transactions and their settlement. … It would balance the positions of large and small traders by offering a neutral trading base and an anonymous process in which several small sellers could meet large buyers." Good idea. This is how the costs and benefits of emission reductions, carbon sinks, and debt swaps can be transacted with efficiency and fairness.

This is not a call for another bureaucracy. The foundations and much of the expertise for an environment bank already exist. The Global Environment Facility, set up in 1991, is a collaboration of UNDP, UNEP, and the World Bank. It is the temporary funding arrangement for the Climate Change Convention, and could be much more than that.

Initiate a virtuous collusion among governments to cut anti-environment subsidies.
UNEP, in its woeful *Outlook 2000*, figured that governments altogether spend more than $700 billion every year "subsidizing environmentally unsound practices in the use of water, agriculture, energy and road transport." Whatever high-minded purposes might have originally justified such subsidies, they invariably develop strong political roots. Their removal is all the more difficult when beneficiaries can threaten to leave the country if subsidies are withdrawn. Governments can improve the environment, and their budgets, by conspiring together in subsidy elimination. If farm communities need support, they can be helped directly – not by subsidies that encourage wasting scarce water or burning high-carbon fuels, but by income supports that actually reward conservation. The conspiracies we recommend do not require big negotiations of the WTO kind; they can start with neighbouring countries, protecting shared environments.

One last, short observation on this subject. Much has been said about NIMBY, or Not In My Backyard, the natural and selfish tendency to want the benefits of a fine environment without enduring the inconveniences. We think the NIMBY syndrome can be turned to a global public good, and a force for democratic governance. After all, some of the world's most toxic environmental

malpractice has been committed in the dictatorships, where NIMBY
had no influence except among the favoured élites. The more
people understand the true costs of the high-carbon economy,
the perils of climate change to themselves and their children, and
the real opportunities for reform, the more they will insist on
achieving that reform. Transparency and accountability in
governance – in every institution of power – will make for better
environment policy. Managing climate change is probably only
possible if the management is democratic.

FINAL WORD

With respect to all three of these imperatives — preventing deadly conflict, providing opportunities for the young, and managing climate change — we acknowledge that our recommendations are for the most part neither revolutionary nor original. They are conventional in almost every detail (to a fault, some will say). But if they were actually carried out, these simple proposals would improve governance in transformative ways. The dynamic opportunities of globalization would be more readily seized, the perils mitigated, and the costs more fairly shared. It is a project for which the UN, as facilitator and coordinator, is uniquely equipped to promote the necessary public–private partnerships.

CONCLUSION
GOVERNING PRINCIPLES:
THE UNITED NATIONS AND
THE MILLENNIUM ASSEMBLY

Globalization surrounds us all in turmoil, and propels our lives through its confusion of contradictions. It empowers some people while it impoverishes others. It celebrates the market and jeopardizes economic growth. It is an engine of invention, a machine of destruction. It liberates and defeats. It invites us to share the pleasures of a common culture while it menaces heritage, tradition, and belief. Globalization mocks the state and demands more of it, validates democracy and subverts it. All our assumptions and institutions of governance are put at risk in its disorder.

In a world of globalization, new ways of governance are needed. We know this, because the old ways are failing. Income disparities are growing much worse. More people are poor. Deadly conflicts cause appalling misery, even when they could be – should be – prevented; weapons of mass destruction threaten us all. The climate, the very future of life on the planet, is in peril. These are the harms and injustices that compel us to remake the ways we govern ourselves.

This is no argument for world government; far from it. The dynamics of globalization itself argue for power decentralized – dispersed to those most affected, and most effective. The guiding rule is to direct energies at the global, regional, national, or domestic levels, and in the networks connecting them, wherever those energies will work best. Indeed, the power structures of the present globalization look more like networks than hierarchies. And the UN system forms a natural nexus to those networks of governance – a knowledge exchange, a place of advocacy and fair hearing, a unique source of legitimacy that gives moral authority to the actions of states. As such, the UN is an invaluable asset in the development of better governance.

Better governance will not come easily. Habits of mind are hard to change, particularly the fatalism that says nothing (or not much) can be done. Any reforming enterprise must also recognize that powerful interests, both public and private, profit in the present circumstances. They will oppose change that threatens them, just as globalization itself inspires resistance among those who fear its effects and suffer its inequities. But the upshot of good governance is a set of bargains in which everybody shares the gains. The penalty of failure could well be a shared catastrophe of violence, scarcity, and destruction.

Much of what is disturbing about globalization – and much of the damage, we have argued – is the sum of the consequences of millions of uncoordinated decisions and actions. The depletion of aquifers, the permanent disemployment of workers, the crash of a currency, the outbreak of a civil war, poisoned air: these are not inevitable or somehow natural occurrences. They are the effects of what men and women do. They represent classic failures of governance (and sometimes failures of markets).

Nor is it naive to think that governance can be reformed. Let it be remembered that at another time of failures and confusion, in 1944, a small group in conservative suits (unlikely revolutionaries) gathered at a New Hampshire resort, took apart the global financial system, and built whole new institutions of governance. Our present is in part a construction of the past. Just as they did at Bretton Woods, we can reconstruct the future.

In designing a different future, we get no direction from the old dogmas. Still less do the old slogans carry conviction. There is no time now for the sanctimonious hectoring that passes for policy when North lectures South. And there is no time left for the self-righteous victimism of the South, where too many bad governments have made excuses for their own bad mistakes. What is needed, if we are to save ourselves from disaster, is first of all straight talk.

But straight talk is not enough without democratic governance. While it is true that most people now live in (more or less) democratic states, it is also true that their lives are now (more and more) governed by nonstate institutions. How democratic is the IMF? CNN? Amnesty International? Reebok? This has been called the democratic deficit — the non-accountability and seeming inaccessibility of intergovernmental organizations, transnational corporations, and those fluid, stateless networks of finance, production, politics, and communications where power is exercised in the global community.

People have a right to a say in the conduct of the institutions that govern their lives. That requires a transparency and responsibility in these institutions of governance, and regulation where appropriate by democratic governments. But democracy also requires the inclusion, in decision-making itself, of those who are affected by the decisions. In the case of intergovernmental organizations (the WTO, for one), that means overcoming the disadvantages suffered especially by people and governments of

the South: creating ombudsman mechanisms, for example, and building stronger capacity in developing countries. These are the people most vulnerable to the decisions of governance, and of misgovernance.

We have tried in these pages not to specify all the answers, but to animate and contribute to an open global debate on these questions. For the prevention of deadly conflict, we have proposed measures to strengthen the UN's capacity to respond to crises, and to alter the politics of a malfunctioning Security Council. We have addressed the desperate urgency of providing opportunities for a billion teenagers, two billion young people in all, and more in the next quarter-century, with better schooling, access to communications, quick improvements in childhood health, and relief from the bondage of debt. And we have recommended the conclusion of a grand bargain, between the rich countries and the poor, to manage global warming and minimize its worst effects. All of these are projects of governance, beyond the competence of any government acting alone. Each places the UN where it belongs in these debates: at the centre.

Next September in Manhattan, at the millennial gathering of the UN General Assembly, debate can become action. This special Assembly can only begin the process of reform, but it should do no less than that. The summit, with the valuable participation of civil society, can itself constitute an exercise in good governance — a democratic and inclusive reconstruction of our future.

But there is a danger. The Assembly and its summit must not be allowed to degenerate into another sterile episode of set speeches and empty promises.

Instead, we recommend a better investment of time, a better use of this extraordinary opportunity. We have proposed some practical actions in the realm of policy change. Now we make another suggestion, this time of summit procedure. We propose that leaders assemble in small groups for several hours of real discussion about the real problems they share. Problems in the three imperatives of governance we've advanced, problems of urbanization or education, transnational crime or ethnic reconciliation, development and environment. Plenty of experience in other summits convinces us that this is what government leaders actually like and need: to dispense with dull texts (and brilliant officials), to be spared pseudo-negotiations over prewritten and unread communiqués, and to engage in the real work of governance in a complicated world. The procedures we recommend would free summit participants to do just that, addressing the problems that interest them in groups of their own choosing. They would also be free (and much more likely) to agree on real action toward more effective and successful governance.

The test of their wisdom, and of the summit itself, will lie in its results. As citizens of the global community, we all confront difficulties, and opportunities, never known before. The difficulties, most of them, have been of our own making. But the opportunities of globalization represent great power, and great promise. It is for us now to determine that the power will be well used, and the promise fulfilled.

APPENDIX 1
SOURCES AND RESOURCES

A suffocating quantity of nonsense and self-promotion has been written about globalization. We are all the more grateful, therefore, to acknowledge the wisdom and insights that have influenced our own thinking in the preparation of this report. What follows is our own short, working guide through the best of the available resources.

A number of reports proved invaluable sources of analysis and data: UNDP's annual *Human Development Report* (Oxford University Press); from UNICEF, *The State of the World's Children 2000* (Oxford University Press) and *The Progress of Nations 1999* (source of Box 3); on connections between environment and health, *World Resources 1998-1999: Environmental Change and Human Health* (Oxford University Press), prepared jointly by the World Resources Institute, UNEP, UNDP, and the World Bank (and the source for Table 1 and Figures 2, 3, and 5); the Final Report of the Carnegie Commission on Preventing Deadly Conflict (and the source for Boxes 1 and 2); the *1999 State of the Future* (American Council for The United Nations University); and *Connecting with the World* (IDRC, International Institute for Sustainable Development, and North–South Institute, 1996), the report of a task force chaired by Maurice Strong, with a useful examination of the interaction between information technology and knowledge-based development. *Our Global Neighborhood* (Oxford University Press), the 1995 Report of the Commission on Global Governance, endures as an extraordinarily far-sighted inquiry into questions of global governance. The authors of all these reports will find their own ideas and advice echoed in our report, and they have our thanks. (Table 2 is reproduced with permission of the Swiss Reinsurance Company.)

Among the scholarly works we found most useful were the following: *Global Transformations* by David Held, Anthony McGrew, David Goldblatt, and Jonathan Perraton (Stanford University

Press, 1999); *Along the Domestic-Foreign Frontier* by James N. Rosenau
(Cambridge University Press, 1997); *Global Public Goods: International
Cooperation in the 21st Century* edited by Inge Kaul, Isabelle Grunberg,
and Marc Stern (Oxford University Press, 1999); and *Environment,
Scarcity, and Violence* by Thomas F. Homer-Dixon (Princeton
University Press, 1999). Intriguing research findings on the
interactions of social science and postconflict peacebuilding are
available from the Geneva-based War-Torn Societies Project
(http://www.unrisd. org/wsp). Hannah Arendt reflected on many
of these questions some 30 years ago in *On Violence* (Harcourt
Brace, 1970). We are also obliged to Joseph S. Nye of Harvard
University for planting the seed, at a Ditchley Park conference,
of our proposal that the UN Secretary-General refer serious
human-rights abuses to the General Assembly.

Some books deserve study because of the stir they cause, and
because of their contribution to the public discourse. Three
among them are Robert D. Kaplan's *The Ends of the Earth* (Random
House, 1995), Benjamin Barber's *Jihad vs. McWorld* (Times Books,
1995), and Thomas L. Friedman's *The Lexus and the Olive Tree*
(Farrar, Straus, Giroux, 1999). For essential reading on how
the world works, we recommend *Foreign Policy*, published
quarterly in several languages (Figures 1 and 4 are from the
summer 1999 and fall 1997 issues, respectively).

Globalization, as we have seen, occurs in a turbulent confluence
of technology, attitude, and ideas. To master the fluid dynamics
of the globalizing culture (or just to acquire a cool new
vocabulary), read three magazines: *Wired, Shift*, and *Fast Company*.
If nothing else, they provide excellent dry-land preparation for
what must come next — surfing the Web.

The Internet is to globalization what the printing press has
been to literacy: cause and effect, medium and message. It is
also a source of good information. The preparation of our
report, for example, was greatly facilitated by the contributions
of scholars from around the globe to a colloquy we started

at http://www.globalcentres.org/un/un.html. The UN
(http://www.un.org) and its agencies have made themselves
admirably accessible on the Web, as have scores of other
intergovernmental organizations. The best place to find them all
is a directory administered at Northwestern University in Chicago
(http://www.library.nwu.edu/govpub/resource/internat/igo.html);
it lists everything from the African Development Bank and the
Asian and Pacific Coconut Community to NATO and the
WTO, with hotlinks to most. Among other reliable sites
we visited: Britain's Overseas Development Institute (http://
www.oneworld.org/odi/) and the UN Foundation (http://www.
unfoundation.org) and its daily bulletin of pertinent news stories
from around the world (http://www.unfoundation.org/unwire).
But this only begins to describe what's available on the Internet;
the offerings are limitless, and grow continuously.

FRIENDS OF THE UNITED NATIONS

While its authors bear all responsibility for the content of this report, it is published on behalf of "Friends of the United Nations: Vision at the Millennium." The Friends were convened by Maureen O'Neil, President of the International Development Research Centre, to advise the authors in the course of their work and to give advice on related and future activities of the UN Foundation and the Better World Fund. The extraordinary contributions of our colleagues among the Friends, in this and so many other endeavours, are hereby acknowledged with admiration and gratitude.

Margaret Catley-Carlson
1790 Broadway, Suite 800
New York, NY 10019, USA

Gordon Conway
President
The Rockefeller Foundation
420 Fifth Avenue
New York, NY 10018-2702, USA

Hans Dahlgren
Swedish Ambassador to the UN
46th Floor, 885 Second Avenue
New York, NY 10017, USA

Francis Deng
Senior Fellow
Brookings Institution
1775 Massachusetts Avenue NW
Washington DC 20036, USA

Mohamed T. El-Ashry
CEO and Chairman
Global Environment Facility
Secretariat
The World Bank,
1818 H Street NW
Washington, DC 20433, USA

Jean-Claude Faby
Vice President
UN Foundation/
Better World Fund
801 Second Avenue, Suite 404
New York, NY 10017, USA

Shepard Forman
Director
Center on International
Cooperation
New York University, Suite 543
418 Lafayette Street
New York, NY 10003, USA

Paul Isenman
Vice President for Programs
UN Foundation
1301 Connecticut Avenue NW,
Suite 700
Washington, DC 20036, USA

Rick R. Little
President and CEO
International Youth Foundation
32 South Street, Suite 500
Baltimore, MD 21202, USA

Edward Luck
Executive Director
Centre for the Study of
International Organizations
New York University
School of Law
Room B45F, Vanderbilt Hall
40 Washington Square South
New York, NY 10012, USA

Princeton Lyman
Overseas Development Council
1875 Connecticut Avenue
Washington, DC 20009, USA

Julia Marton-Lefèvre
Executive Director
Leadership for Environment
and Development (LEAD)
International
700 Broadway, 3rd Floor
New York, NY 10003, USA

Kishore Mahbubani
Singapore Ambassador to the UN
231 East 51st Street
New York, NY 10022, USA

Moisés Naím
Editor, *Foreign Policy*
Carnegie Endowment for
International Peace
1778 Massachusetts Avenue NW
Washington, DC 20036, USA

Moeen A. Qureshi
Chairman
Emerging Markets Corporation
2001 Pennsylvania Avenue, NW,
Suite 1100
Washington, DC 20006, USA

Gita Rau Gupta
President
International Center for Research
on Women
1717 Massachusetts Avenue, NW,
Suite 302
Washington, DC 20036, USA

Wolfgang Reinicke
Senior Economist
The World Bank
Room MC8-771
1818 H Street NW
Washington, DC 20433, USA

Emma Rothschild
Director
Center for History and Economics
Kings College
Cambridge CB2 1ST, UK

Pierre Sané
Amnesty International
1 Easton Street
London WC1X 8DG, UK

Klaus Schwab
President
World Economic Forum
53, chemin des Hauts-Crêts
1223 Geneva, Switzerland

Ismail Serageldin
Vice President
Special Programs,
The World Bank
Room MC 4132,
1818 H Street NW
Washington, DC 20433, USA

Gordon Smith
2027 Runnymede Avenue
Victoria, BC, Canada V8S 2V5

Rehman Sobhan
President
Centre for Policy Dialogue
6/A Eskaton Garden
Ramna, Dhaka 1000, Bangladesh

John Stremlau
Professor
Department of International
Relations
University of the Witwatersrand
Private Bag 3, WITS 2050,
South Africa

Maurice Strong
Chairman of the Executive
Committee
UN Foundation
1301 Connecticut Avenue, NW,
Suite 700
Washington, DC 20036, USA

Brian Urquhart
50 West 29th Street
New York, NY 10001, USA

Oscar Vieira
Executive Secretary
Ilanud/Brasil
R. Dr. Vila Nova, 268, 3o. andar
São Paulo, Brazil

Timothy Wirth
President
UN Foundation
1301 Connecticut Avenue, NW,
Suite 700
Washington, DC 20036, USA

Ex Officio Observers

Patrizio Civili
Assistant Secretary-General
for Policy Coordination and
Inter-Agency Affairs
UN Department for Economic
and Social Affairs
Two United Nations Plaza
Room DC2-2308
New York, NY 10017, USA

Louise Fréchette
Deputy Secretary-General
Executive Office of the
Secretary-General
United Nations, Room S-3860A
New York, NY 10017, USA

Andrew Mack
Director, Strategic Planning Unit
Executive Office of the
Secretary-General
United Nations, Room S-3860A
New York, NY 10017, USA

John Gerard Ruggie
Assistant Secretary-General
Executive Office of the
Secretary-General
United Nations, Room S-3860A
New York, NY 10017, USA

Mark Malloch Brown
Administrator
United Nations Development
Programme
One United Nations Plaza
Room 2128
New York, NY 10017, USA

Shashi Tharoor
Director of Communications
and Special Projects
United Nations, Room S-3802D
New York, NY 10017, USA

LIST OF ACRONYMS

AIDS   acquired immune deficiency syndrome

CDM   Clean Development Mechanism

HIV   human immunodeficiency virus

IMF   International Monetary Fund

NATO   North Atlantic Treaty Organization

NGO   nongovernmental organization

NIMBY   Not In My Backyard

OECD   Organisation for Economic Co-operation and Development

UN   United Nations

UNDP   United Nations Development Programme

UNEP   United Nations Environment Programme

UNICEF   United Nations Children's Fund

WHO   World Health Organization

WTO   World Trade Organization

THE AUTHORS, THE PUBLISHER, AND THE SPONSOR

Gordon Smith is Director of the Centre for Global Studies at the University of Victoria and a Senior Fellow in the Liu Centre at the University of British Columbia, Canada. He is Chairman of the Board of Governors of Canada's International Development Research Centre and the Canadian Institute for Climate Studies, and directs the Canadian Global Change Program. Previously, Dr Smith was Deputy Minister of Foreign Affairs and Personal Representative of the Prime Minister of Canada for the G7 and G8 summits. He has also served Canada as its Ambassador to NATO and as its Deputy Minister of Social Development. Dr Smith was educated at McGill University and received his doctorate from the Massachusetts Institute of Technology.

Moisés Naím is the Editor of *Foreign Policy* magazine. He has written extensively on the political economy of international trade and investment, multilateral organizations, economic reforms, and on globalization. He is the author or editor of eight books and of numerous articles. Dr Naím served as Venezuela's Minister of Trade and Industry and played a central role in the initial launching of major economic reforms in 1989. Preceding his ministerial position, Dr Naím served as Professor and Dean at the Instituto de Estudios Superiores de Administración in Caracas. Between 1992 and 1996, he was the Director of the Projects on Economic Reforms and on Latin America at the Carnegie Endowment for International Peace in Washington, DC. Dr Naím has also been associated with the World Bank, first as an executive director and some years later as Senior Adviser to the President. Dr Naím holds doctorate and master's degrees from the Massachusetts Institute of Technology.

Canada's **International Development Research Centre** (IDRC) is committed to building a sustainable and equitable world. IDRC funds developing-world researchers, thus enabling the people of the South to find their own solutions to their own problems. IDRC also maintains information networks and forges linkages that allow Canadians and their developing-world partners to benefit equally from a global sharing of knowledge. Through its actions, IDRC is helping others to help themselves.

IDRC Books publishes research results and scholarly studies on global and regional issues related to sustainable and equitable development. As a specialist in development literature, IDRC Books contributes to the body of knowledge on these issues to further the cause of global understanding and equity. IDRC publications are sold through its head office in Ottawa, Canada, as well as by IDRC's agents and distributors around the world. The full catalogue is available at http://www.idrc.ca/books/index.html.

This study was funded by the **Better World Fund**, sister organization to the United Nations Foundation. The two organizations were established to support the goals and objectives of the United Nations, with special emphasis on the UN's work on behalf of economic, social, environmental, and humanitarian causes. This study has been prepared as part of the "UN Vision" project; this project aims to help strengthen the United Nations to act increasingly effectively and efficiently in this new and constantly changing environment in order to promote a more peaceful, prosperous, and just world.